Rotations in Stability Operations

EXECUTIVE SUMMARY

Title: THE UNITED STATES CULTURE OF ROTATIONAL WARFARE

Author: MAJ Gregory Gibbons, United States Army

Thesis: Conducting stability operations using unit rotations is a self-defeating system that instills a negative mindset in military leaders and works in favor of the U.S. adversary by prolonging the conflict.

Discussion: Military theorists, such as Carl von Clausewitz, argue against involvement in protracted warfare because it works in favor of the less-powerful enemy. Al Qaida doctrine argues successful terrorists must prolong the conflict in order to exhaust the United States, its allies, their treasure, and their will to fight. For the past eleven years, military service members have been involved in rotational warfare, which has hindered their ability to end the conflicts quickly. Rotational warfare limits the forces available for post conflict stability operations and counterinsurgency operations, hinders continuity, negatively affects the mindset of leaders, and inevitably prolongs the conflict. Sending troops into stability operations until they achieve the endstate rather than rotating them allows the military to use overwhelming presence, successfully handle post conflict stability operations and counterinsurgency operations, maintain continuity, uphold a mission-accomplishment objective mindset in military leaders, and avoid protracted warfare.

Conclusion: In order to avoid protracted warfare, U.S. leaders should not use rotational warfare. U.S. military leaders must deploy a force that provides an overwhelming presence in the area of operations with the mission to achieve the endstate.

Acknowledgments

To my wife, Shelli, whose dedicated support has allowed me to perform a job I love. Thank you for providing unending editorial support and allowing me to drive you crazy with this research project for the last year.

To Dr. Jonathan Phillips for all the hours spent discussing, reviewing, advising, and directing this project, without your mentoring this paper would be little more than an unremarkable idea.

To the United States Army who allowed me the opportunity to attended the Marine Corps Command And Staff College and this time to think, read, and write.

Table of Contents

DISCLAIMER

THE OPINIONS AND CONCLUSIONS EXPRESSED HEREIN ARE THOSE OF THE
INDIVIDUAL STUDENT AUTHOR AND DO NOT NECESSARILY REPRESENT THE VIEWS
OF EITHER THE MARINE COPS COMMAND AND STAFF COLLEGE OR ANY OTHER
GOVERNMENTAL AGENCY. REFERENCES TO THIS STUDY SHOULD INCLUDE THE
FOREGOING STATEMENT.

QUOTATION FROM, ABSTRACTION FROM, OR REPRODUCTION OF ALL OR ANY PART
OF THIS DOCUMENT IS PERMITTED PROVIDED PROPER ACKNOWLEDGEMENT IS
MADE.

"Units and their leaders cannot be rotated out after short tours, which will strain force structure and possibly degrade combat readiness. The nation and the Army must be prepared to commit considerable time, manpower, and money to make an occupation of Iraq successful in the long term."[1]

> Reconstructing Iraq, February 2003
> (The reconstruction plan developed by the Army War College and DAG3 Staff before the invasion of Iraq)

Introduction

The United States military is the dominant force in the world today. No adversary can meet U.S. forces head to head on the battlefield and succeed. Protracted war is the only method an opposing force can use to overcome the U.S. military. Protracted warfare exhausts the will of the American people and their treasure. Three protracted wars in the past 50 years of U.S. history all had one thing in common. The conflicts in Vietnam, Afghanistan, and Iraq all used rotational warfare. In Vietnam, individuals rotated in and out of theater. In Afghanistan and Iraq, entire units rotated in and out of the fight. In this system of rotational warfare, one-third of the force deployed to the conflict, one-third of the force remained home to train for the conflict, and one-third of the force returned home and recovered from the conflict.

With only one-third of the force available to fight, rotational warfare limits the forces available for post conflict and counterinsurgency operations. Rotating units in and out of the fight hinders continuity, negatively affects the mindset of leaders, and alters the way they use their resources. Ultimately, rotational warfare prolongs the length of the post conflict stability operations and allows otherwise powerless adversaries a chance to turn stability operations into a protracted insurgency. U.S. leaders should send individuals and military units to post conflict stability operations until they achieve the endstate rather than rotating them in and out. This would allow the military to use all of the available fighting force, successfully handle post conflict stability and counterinsurgency operations, maintain continuity, uphold an endstate-objective mindset in military leaders, and avoid protracted warfare.

This paper will explain the importance of avoiding protracted warfare. It will show how rotational warfare leads to protracted warfare and will address three main issues with using rotations. The first issue will address availability of troops during security and post conflict stability operations. The second issue will focus on lack of advisor continuity and unit continuity during rotations. The third issue will identify a negative mindset in troops and leaders caused by rotational warfare. Service members understand these three issues are caused by rotations.

This paper moves forward to address solutions with this understood problem. It will examine strategies used in past wars, including the theory of "overwhelming force" used in the 1991 Persian Gulf War. The paper will argue that the same strategy of "overwhelming force" could be adapted to "overwhelming presence" during post conflict stability and counterinsurgency operations to avoid protracted warfare. This paper will then conclude by addressing three counter arguments to the elimination of rotational warfare; troop morale, recruiting shortfalls, and hardships to military families.

This paper is not intended to be a solution for Iraq, Afghanistan, or every conflict. The purpose of this paper is to address the importance of preparing for post conflict stability operations. It demonstrates the importance of getting post conflict stability operations correct in order to avoid an insurgency. While making future leaders aware of the negative effects of rotational warfare, this paper informs the current generation of war fighters, who only know OEF and OIF rotational warfare, that rotational warfare is not the only option available for planners of future operations. This paper proposes one option for consideration that will eliminate the negative effects of rotational warfare and avoid protracted warfare.

Protracted Warfare

Military theorist, Carl von Clausewitz, addressed the importance of time and treasure in war. Clausewitz argues the will of the people to fight a war is primordial violence. Primordial violence represents how much blood and treasure the people are willing to give for the cause.[2] The government and military can only continue to fight as long as the will of the people lasts. The longer the war continues and the more treasure that is spent, the more the will of the people fades. Adversaries know this. U.S. leaders know that adversaries know this. U.S. military doctrine states, "[Enemies know] they cannot compete with U.S. forces… Instead, they try to exhaust U.S. national will, aiming to win by undermining and outlasting public support"[3] (Field Manual 3-24, Counterinsurgency). Primordial violence wanes with protracted wars and adversaries such as Al Qaida are not shy about using the theory to their advantage.

Norman Cigar analyzed Al Qaida's strategy for fighting stronger state governments and militaries. Cigar analyzes the writing of Abd Al-Aziz Al Murqurin, the one time leader of Al Qaida for the Arab Peninsula. In Al Murqurin's, *A Practical Course for Guerrilla War*, Cigar finds that Al Murqurin studied Clausewitz and Mao.[4] Cigar also finds that Al Murqurin's strategy for guerrilla war is "characterized by protracted combat intended to exhaust the enemy."[5] Al Murqurin envisioned a guerrilla war in Saudi Arabia lasting twenty to thirty years.[6] The ideas written in Al Murqurin's book are the doctrine used by Al Qaida today. Author Daveed Gartenstein-Ross quotes the methodology of Al Qaida, which states "Hand in hand, we will be with you until you are bankrupt and your economy collapses."[7] Al Qaida's strategy to win against the U.S. is to protract the conflict in order to exhaust the will of the people and U.S. treasure.

The U.S. Army identified protracted warfare as the one vulnerability weaker forces can exploit. Theorists call attention to this weakness and advise leaders to avoid prolonged conflict.[8] Weaker forces use protracted warfare to exhaust the will of the people. Even Al Qaida is aware of the advantages of prolonged warfare and instructs followers to implement it as a strategy. If the U.S. military knows protracted warfare is its weakness, theorists warn against getting involved in it, and U.S. enemies knowingly employ it as a strategy, then why would U.S. leaders allow protracted wars to occur? Yet, the current system of rotational warfare is creating the exact situation U.S. strategists should be avoiding, protracted warfare.

"Combat Power is the total destructive force we can bring to bear on our enemy at a given time. Some factors in combat power are quite tangible and easily measured such as superior numbers, which Clausewitz called "the most common element in victory."[9]

MCDP 1 Warfighting, 1997

Rotational Warfare

Rotational warfare hinders the ability of the U.S. military to fight by only allowing 33% of the fighting force to deploy. The system of deploying units to combat using rotations is with a two to one ratio. The Army Rotation Rule Project (TARRP) defines this ratio as the "Rule of 3." The Rule of 3 dictates that "three units are committed to each operation—one training for the operation, one deployed to the operation, and one recovering from the operation."[10] The rotational method of warfare immediately cuts the force before the conflict has begun.[11] Using rotational warfare eliminates 66% of the forces available to planners when developing strategies for conducting the post conflict stability operations. During post conflict stability operations, this is especially detrimental.

Rotational Issue #1: Troop Availability

The first issue with using rotational warfare is limited troop availability when conducting

post conflict stability and counterinsurgency operations. When combat operations end, warfare

moves into post conflict stability operations. In an interview with Brigadier General H.R.

McMaster who commanded the 3rd Armored Cavalry Regiment in Tal Afar, Iraq in 2005, the

importance of troop numbers becomes clear. McMaster argues the priority of the military in post

conflict stability operations is to "set the security conditions for economic, political development,

development of additional security forces" and to set the stage for "Rule of Law."

> "Yeah, the number of troops matters… if you do not have enough troops
> you then have to assume risk in certain areas…You do less simultaneous
> activity and you do more sequential activity. What that effect will
> specifically do is protract the campaign and it can also allow the enemy to
> retain safe havens and support bases which makes it difficult even to hold
> onto areas you have cleared."[12]

In 2005, McMaster conducted Operation RESTORING RIGHTS, which quelled insurgents in

Tal Afar by showing a lasting presence of military troops in the city and gaining credibility

among the locals.

Using overwhelming presence in post conflict stability operations is one way to ensure

that security operations are successful and an insurgency does not begin. The first six to twelve

weeks following combat operations are crucial.[13] The occupation force must provide the basic

needs to the host nation populace. Basic needs include security from uprisings and criminal

activity and the restoration of basic services of medical, food, and water. Once this is

established, the military can pass over duties and responsibilities to Other Governmental

Agencies (OGA), Non Governmental Organizations (NGO), humanitarian aid workers, charity

organizations, and a host nation government. The failure to provide these basic needs to the

local population will result in an uprising against the occupying force and an insurgency.

Civilian organizations will not be able to enter the theater and the military will have to conduct counterinsurgency operations and nation building alone. Insights from past conflicts in Panama, Haiti, and Germany highlight the importance of troop numbers to conduct security and reconstruction operations.

In a study conducted in preparation for the invasion of Iraq in 2003, the Army War College and the Army Staff reviewed the reconstruction efforts from stability operations in Panama and Haiti. The study found troop numbers contributed to the success and failure of the operations. In Panama, the study found that military policemen "were inadequate in numbers to deal with the problems they faced in the aftermath" of the combat operations. [14] In Haiti, the study found that the "overwhelming force deployed in the initial occupation and the soldiers' professional and disciplined conduct and appearance in continuing operations did much to deter and control the actions of potential troublemakers."[15] An "overwhelming presence" was essential to the initial success in Haiti and an "inadequate" number of troops was detrimental in Panama.

While it is difficult to determine exactly how many troops make up an "overwhelming presences," the U.S. military does have an idea of how many troops are necessary for security operations. The U.S. manual on counterinsurgency states "successful COIN operations often require a high ratio of security forces to the protected population."[16] A "high ratio of security forces" stresses the importance of boots on the ground. Operations and Field Manual 3-24 lays out the ratio of security forces to populace as 20 to 25 security forces for every 1,000 inhabitants.[17] If the population of the host nation is ten million then the U.S. military will need at least 200,000 troops for security alone. Additional troops will be required for other missions, such as the advisory and mentorship rolls. Numbers this high ensure an "overwhelming presence" is able to maintain security and succeed in post conflict stability operations. Yet, the current system of rotational warfare limits the number of troops available and forces the military to make the mission work without an adequate number of soldiers.

Lessons learned from the reconstruction of Germany after World War II also show the importance of overwhelming troop numbers following combat operations. Security of the German people was the first U.S. step towards rebuilding Germany. Patrols, check points, and border protection by the U.S. military ensured that everyone knew and understood who was in control and in charge.[18] American forces protected the German people from crime by providing law and order. This early management of security by a large number of forces allowed the U.S. military to focus on the rebuilding of Germany.

If the U.S. military does not deploy a force that can handle the key moments after combat operations the result will be an insurgency, civilian organizations will not enter the theater, and the conflict will become protracted. With an overwhelming number of troops available, U.S. military leaders can ensure troop numbers are available to secure the populace, provide basic services, and hand over responsibility to civilian organizations as quickly as possible. Rotational warfare limits the amount of troops available for post conflict stability and increases the chance that security will fail, insurgencies arise, and a protracted war begins.

The failure to provide security immediately after defeating a military force will lead to a second conflict against an insurgency. This insurgency will be a more organized, better supplied, and supported resistance. When violence erupts and the insurgency gains a foothold, civilian organizations cannot enter the theater and the military must take on the rolls of advisor and mentor. As advisor and mentor, the military must stand up and advise a host nation government, build and mentor a host nation military, rebuild basic services, and gain security.

Lessons learned in past counterinsurgency operations call attention to the importance of continuity in advisory and mentorship rolls.

Rotational Issue # 2: Advisory and Unit Continuity

The second issue with using rotational warfare is poor advisory and unit continuity. The success the British had in fighting a counterinsurgency in Malaya highlights the importance of advisory continuity. Captain Jeanne F. Hull from the Strategic Studies Institute cites Sir Robert Thompson who argued British success in fighting a counterinsurgency in the Malayan Emergency was a result of advisory continuity with key personnel who worked with the insurgents[19] and the established Malayan government.[20] Hull recognized the success in Malaya and compared it to the Force Strategic Engagement Cell (FSEC) experience in Iraq. Hull argued the "FSEC rotation cycle…was not conducive to the continuity" of relationships with Iraqi government personnel, tribal shaykhs, and insurgent group representatives.[21] Hull argued entire projects that took months of work with key Iraqi leaders were lost when personnel rotated. The new personnel were unable to reestablish continuity because the Iraqi personnel did not have a relationship with the new advisor. Hull recommended a period of *at least* two years for advisors.

Units in the U.S. military rotate into conflicts at different intervals depending on the branch of service and the unit. During much of the war in Iraq, U.S. Marine Corps units rotated every seven months, while units in the U.S. Army rotated every twelve to fifteen months. The rotation timeline did not give advisors the minimum two-year period that Hull argues is necessary. In addition, the rotation itself hindered continuity of information for advisors. Brigadier General H. R. McMaster argues there was a loss of key information when new units rotated into theater.

"We had to call the 101st at Campbell and say, "Hey man, will you put all your SIPR (Secret Internet Protocol Router) stuff from Nineveh Province back up on the server so we could access it because nobody had any of it…any of their reporting, any of their assessments, anything…That's a good example of a very poor hand off…loss of all the knowledge that had been fought for. We had to fight for the same information twice."[22]

McMaster's experience shows that units had trouble ensuring advisory continuity during rotations. McMaster's went on to say, "That's an example of how screwed up it could be. I don't think anyone wanted to screw that up but it was just that."[23] Regardless of the length of the rotation, rotational warfare significantly hinders the ability for key personnel to maintain continuity in advisory and mentorship rolls and ultimately helps to prolong the operation.

The Vietnam War also exemplifies the detrimental effect of rotations on advisory continuity. John Paul Vann, Army Lieutenant Colonel and civilian advisor in Vietnam from 1962 to 1974 argued, "We don't have twelve years' experience in the country. We have one year's experience twelve times."[24] Like McMaster, Vann's experience was that of lack of continuity between advisors, but another problem with rotations was that of prolonged effectiveness of each new advisor. Edward Metzner, who served three tours as an advisor in Vietnam, stated, "By the time each advisor was beginning to learn how to function effectively, his year was up and he went home."[25] In Vietnam, this was particularly evident for battalion level advisors and below, where tour lengths were usually six months.[26] In 1965, a RAND Corporation study on the U.S. advisory effort from 1945-1965 suggested a period from six to eight months as the break-in period for advisors.[27] With a twelve month rotation cycle some Vietnamese commanders had 26 U.S. advisors during the war, each with four to six months of truly productive mentorship. The rotational system in Vietnam clearly hindered advisory continuity and worked against advisory goals.

In Operation IRAQI FREEDOM (OIF) and Operation ENDURING FREEDOM (OEF) units conducted a two week Transfer of Authority to hand over equipment and knowledge to the incoming unit. In Iraq, this short, two week period created breaks in advisory continuity and relationships with Iraqi forces. Army Lieutenant Colonel Francis Parks argued, "These breaks would hinder U.S. Forces from sustaining progress in developing Iraqi units in a culture markedly different from that of their U.S. conventional unit partners and advisors."[28] In two weeks, even the best units could not transfer relationships effectively. Parks described what an effective transfer should be.

> "An advisory effort, once instituted, requires continuity of the relationships between the advisors and the host nation unit counterparts. The system used to source advisors must posture the advisors for success, and protect the continuity of relationship upon which any successful advisory effort depends. These relationships are a necessary requirement, as the end state of any successful advisory effort is for the advisors to have worked themselves out of a job."[29]

The advisory "system" Parks described emphasizes continuity and working toward the endstate. In rotational warfare, Transfer of Authority, not the endstate is the ultimate goal. It is a cycle that inevitably creates protracted warfare.

Unit continuity is also a problem in rotational warfare. When one unit rotates out and another unit rotates in, there is no incentive for the new unit to continue the methodology of the old unit. A new unit arrives with new leaders, new ideas, and new ways of attacking the same problem. Captain Jeanne Hull highlights this rotational issue in the article, "Iraq: Strategic Reconciliation, Targeting, and Key Leader engagements." Hull states, "Unfortunately, when [the incoming unit] rolled into town to replace [the outgoing unit], the [new unit] shut down every major engagement plan and program we had set up."[30] Hull's example was not an isolated event.

Many Brigade Combat Teams (BCT) that rotate into the war determine that their operational plan is better than the one of the unit they replaced. With this type of mindset, units are then responsible for completing their objectives before they rotate out because they cannot expect new units to continue with their plans. It takes between three to six months for a new unit to become fully productive in the war, which means a unit only has six to nine months to execute plans to completion. Add to that any risk aversion mindsets and the timeframe becomes even shorter. In this way, rotational warfare hinders unit continuity, prevents leaders from accomplishing most strategic objectives, and ultimately, prolongs the war.

Rotational Issue # 3: Negative Mindset

The third issue with rotational warfare is a negative mindset among troops and leaders. Just as rotations work against advisory and unit continuity, the system of rotational warfare works against the mindset of troops and military leaders. In a war where the objective is always the endstate, leaders work toward achieving that goal so they may go home. In a war where rotations occur, leaders' objectives change from accomplishing an endstate to getting through a twelve-month deployment. Leaders conducting rotational warfare are risk averse and often mismanage manpower, assets, and money. These negative mindsets work in favor of the adversary and help to prolong the war.

In a "survive twelve months" mentality, leaders and troops know they have a mission in the war, but are guaranteed a redeployment home at the end of their rotation whether they meet the endstate of that mission or not. Leaders and troops make decisions based on this fact. Leaders may assume that a future unit will reach the endstate during their rotation and therefore, prevent putting their own soldiers at risk. As the end of the deployment draws near this risk adverse mentality is quickly recognized. The incoming unit is left to handle the riskier missions

passed over by the departing unit. The same risk aversion can exist in the mind of an individual

soldier, which was the case in the Vietnam War.

Risk aversion was rampant in the Vietnam War. As soldiers neared the end of a rotation

in Vietnam, they became less combat effective because they were reluctant to take risks.[31] In a

study of rotations and counterinsurgency in Vietnam, Lieutenant Colonel Francis Parks found

that "Some units sent troops to the rear earlier, trying to derail what would become known as

"short-timer's syndrome." Parks argued "These projected losses further eroded the effective

strength of a unit, as commanders were often unwilling to unnecessarily risk the lives of troops

about to return home."[32] In Vietnam, "short-timer's syndrome" affected decisions based on

individuals, but in other wars, "short-timer's syndrome" affected decisions based on entire units.

In World War II Germany, troops did not have rotational redeployments to look forward

to. Army Major Dick Winters, made famous in the book *Band of Brothers*, exemplifies the

mentality of a leader not affected by risk aversion. Winters led troops in Echo Company 101st

Airborne Division to accomplish amazing feats. Making difficult decisions and giving orders

that put troops in danger, Winters' goal was to reach the endstate of defeating the Germans.

Many of those decisions and orders risked Winters' life and the lives of his troops, sometimes

leading to their deaths. As the end of the war dawned and the German army was close to defeat,

Winters received orders to conduct patrols in the unit's area of operation. Winters became risk

averse. Winters disobeyed the orders because as the war was ending, he did not want to risk the lives of his troops.[33] Although the mission to defeat the Germans had not changed, Winters'

mindset had changed to getting as many men home alive as possible.

In warfare, even great leaders are at the mercy of a risk aversion mentality. Their

mission may be to defeat the enemy, secure an area, or rebuild a country, but when leaders start

that mission knowing they have an opportunity to bring troops home safely after twelve months

they are less likely to take risks. The troops within the unit also become risk averse, knowing

they have a chance to return home. This makes entire units ineffective towards the end of their

rotation. Rotational warfare creates a mindset of risk aversion before boots even hit the ground,

which ultimately leads to a protracted conflict.

Rotational warfare also negatively affects the mindset of leaders in regards to managing

manpower, assets, and money. When conducting rotational warfare, leaders base decisions on

short-term comforts rather than long-term strategic objectives. They make choices based on the

morale of the soldiers rather than achieving the strategic endstate. In many cases, troops and

assets are used for non-essential tasks rather than missions focused on reaching an endstate.

While these tasks may improve the quality of life for deployed service members, they also

detract from the goal at hand and ultimately help to prolong the war.

In Afghanistan and Iraq, Forward Operating Bases (FOB) became what some describe as

"self-licking ice cream cones." Many FOBs throughout both theaters had giant gymnasiums,

dining facilities, Morale, Welfare, and Recreational (MWR) facilities, as well as an abundance of

fast food and other non-essential stores. In some cases, civilian contractors were hired to build and maintain the facilities, but in other cases, U.S. service members built, operated, and maintained them. U.S. military logistic units transported the supplies, military engineers built the facilities, and military service members operated and maintained them. Even civilian-run entities relied on U.S. military assets. Burger King, for instance, does not have its own trucks, aircraft, or forklifts to bring burgers and fries to FOBs.[34] U.S. military airplanes flew in supplies, military convoys escorted drivers and their loads, and military warehouses stocked all of the supplies to build, maintain, and resupply the facilities. Instead of performing tasks that could help the U.S. meet endstate objectives, military service members were tasked with creating these "self-licking ice cream cones." If redeployment was not expected in a rotational interval, but only occurred when endstate objectives were met, leaders would have to use manpower and assets on fighting the war instead of wasting it on non-essential comforts.

When the U.S. military cannot fulfill all FOB requests, the Army Material Command (AMC) hires Logistics Civil Augmentation Program (LOGCAP) contractors who will. In 2008, AMC signed a LOGCAP contract for $15 billion. The development of LOGCAP was to replace logistics that a downsized military could no longer provide for itself. The development of LOGCAP was not to provide better service to the military. In Iraq, Joint Base Balad took pride in its two swimming pools (indoor and outdoor), one brick movie theater, recreation centers, and high quality mess halls.[35] When civilian contractors perform the work necessary to provide such amenities, money is wasted on frivolities that could otherwise be spent on vital combat expenses instead. This waste of manpower and money exhausts the resources of the military and the treasure of the United States, playing directly into the strategy of the enemy.

In Afghanistan in 2009, International Security Assistance Force (ISAF) Commander, General Stanley McChrystal recognized the wasteful management of money, manpower, and assets. McChrystal gave orders to close down many restaurants. Many service members believed doing away with these amenities was an attempt to make deployments harder. McChrystal attempted to fight against the negative mindset of rotational warfare and refocus assets on the mission. Command Sergeant Major Hall agreed, stating that closure of the facilities opened up much needed logistics assets, storage space, and transportation vehicles for the surge in troops.[36] General McChrystal also recognized the "survive twelve months" mentality and tried to refocus leaders on achieving the endstate.[37] McChrystal redirected money, manpower, and assets "to focus on the war."[38] The mindset derived from rotational warfare is difficult for leaders up the chain to get away from. The only way to address the negative effects of a rotational mindset is to deploy to combat with one focus and that is to achieve a clearly defined military endstate.

Rotational warfare affects the mindset of leaders and service members. It causes leaders and troops to focus on surviving through the deployment instead of reaching an endstate. The rotational mindset also influences leaders to mismanage manpower, money, and assets. War by itself is a costly endeavor. Fighting in an operation that rotates units only increases the cost. The logistics expenses incurred by rotating equipment and forces around the world are enormous and are taking away badly needed funds from vital combat expenses. The negative effects of rotational warfare on the mindset of leaders and service members lead to the misuse of resources and ultimately, protract the war. Deploying units to combat that will only redeploy after meeting the endstate objective of a strategic plan will refocus the mindset of leaders and service members onto fighting and winning the war at hand.

"Rebuilding Iraq will require a considerable commitment of American resources, but the longer U.S. presence is maintained, the more likely violent resistance will develop."[39]

> Reconstructing Iraq, February 2003
> (The reconstruction plan developed by the Army War College and DAG3 Staff before the invasion of Iraq)

Historical Examples

In 2003, during the buildup to Operation IRAQI FREEDOM (OIF), U.S. Secretary of Defense, Donald Rumsfeld, attempted to achieve the Bush administration's goals with a small force and superior technology. Chief of Staff of the Army, General Eric Shinseki argued against using a smaller force. Shinseki stressed the importance of using an overwhelming force, especially in post conflict stability.[40] Shinseki was of the belief that it is better to deploy the full might of the U.S. military initially and drawdown rather than the reverse.[41] Shinseki argued that there was a crucial period after the fall of the Iraq regime when the potential for disorder was enormous. The effects of years to come depended on what happened in those first days and weeks after the regime fell.[42] Without enough troops available, strategists would not be able to implement plans to counter disorder.

Shinseki's argument relied on the knowledge of the Army War College. James Fallows describes the position of the War College stating, "It [is] best to go in heavier than you actually [need] to be, so that at the beginning of the postwar period your presence [will] be so intimidating that nobody would dare challenge you." [43] Rumsfeld disagreed with Shinseki's argument and the conflict began in 2003 with 67,700 troops. The population of Iraq was about 30 million.[44] With a security forces ratio, as stated earlier, of 20 to 25 soldiers for every 1,000 inhabitants, the war should have begun with a minimum of 600,000 troops. Disorder ensued after the regime change in OIF and without enough troops to confront it, the mistake prolonged the war. The following year, troop levels reached 130,600 and by the height of the conflict in

2008, there were 187,900 boots on the ground. Because of the 33% ratio for rotational warfare, troop numbers never reached the minimum number necessary for security, let alone advisory and mentorship rolls. Rotational warfare in OIF did not allow the military to maximize the full strength of the force when it conducted post conflict security and counterinsurgency operations.

During counterinsurgency operations, rotational deployments hindered continuity. U.S. Air Force units rotated in and out of theater every three months and later, every six months. U.S. Marine Corps units rotated every seven months and U.S. Army units rotated every twelve months at the beginning of the war, every fifteen months later in the war, and finally ended on a nine-month rotation schedule.[45] Each time a unit rotated into theater it had to re-establish rapport with the local nationals and begin working on its plan to achieve strategic objectives.

Officially ending on December 18, 2011, the war in Iraq lasted eight years and nine months. All wars are costly, but according to the Brookings Institution, the price tag of OIF was about $1 trillion for the United States.[46] Primordial violence for the war did not last to the end of the war. Rotational warfare exhausted both time and treasure, working against the U.S. military and working to the advantage of the enemy. Also known as the "Second Gulf War," OIF was a costly, protracted war that could have had a much different outcome if rotational warfare had not been used.

Although it did not include an invasion of Iraq, the "First" Gulf War in 1991 had a very different outcome. Chairman of the Joint Chiefs of Staff, General Colin Powell, exercised a strategy during the Persian Gulf War that he also emphasized in unofficial writings known as the Powell Doctrine.[47] During the Persian Gulf War, Powell used an overwhelming number of coalition forces to defeat the Iraqi military. Powell's method was to maximize resources to achieve a decisive force against the enemy, making the weaker force capitulate and ending the conflict quickly.[48] The plan worked and the war lasted less than one year. Troops however, did not know beforehand how long the fight would last and expected to stay as long as necessary. Service members and their leaders upheld a mission-accomplishment objective mindset and continually focused manpower and assets on reaching the endstate.

The endstate of the Persian Gulf War was to push and keep Iraq out of Kuwait and while the endstate of Operation IRAQI FREEDOM was a regime change in Iraq, the methods used in the First Gulf War would have allowed similar successes. The concept of the Powell Doctrine's "overwhelming force" should have been adapted for post conflict stability and counterinsurgency operations in IRAQI FREEDOM. With no troops on the home-front to replace them, troops in the fight of IRAQI FREEDOM would have maintained continuity and an endstate-objective mindset. Future operations should use the "overwhelming force" concept for post conflict stability operations and avoid rotational warfare.

"H. R. McMaster, whose 3rd Armored Cavalry Regiment was principally responsible for clearing insurgent presence out of Tal Afar in 2005, gave "until it's done" as the most appropriate time to withdraw a unit, but also cited "limits of human endurance."[49]

> Major Francis J. H. Parks, *The Unit and the Individual: A Study of Rotation Forces in Counterinsurgency*

Counter Argument

There are several issues that arise when considering a departure from the current system of rotational warfare. Would service members be able to fight effectively if a conflict continued until achieving the endstate? Would there be shortfalls in military recruiting in an "all-volunteer military"? Would non-rotational deployments negatively affect family members of deployed service members? Each question is addressable by looking at past deployments and studies.

Are troops able to handle a lengthy deployment? Over the past ten years of operations in OEF and OIF the military services have studied the effects on troops and their families. From these studies and mission requirements, policy makers have changed the timeframe of deployment rotations in the Army, Marines, and the Air Force several times.[50] None of these studies looked into deploying units and personnel indefinitely. None of these studies addressed the stress on a service member and their family after returning home, while knowing there would be a future deployment in twelve months. What are the effects on military readiness when not conducting rotations compared to ten years of prolonged deployment to OIF and OEF? This is what future studies should focus on.

Will the U.S. military be able to maintain recruiting goals? A look at the history of the "all-volunteer military" in the United States shows that this should not be an issue. The "All Volunteer Military" program began with President Nixon's campaign promise to end the draft in 1968. In 1970, the Gates commission report put the "All Volunteer Army" plan into effect. In 1983, Secretary of Defense Casper Weinberger declared the all-volunteer force program a success and was no longer experimental.[51] From 1970 until the first major combat operations in 1991, the U.S. military operated solely off of the all-volunteer military. If "called up," volunteers had no reason to believe the deployment would not last until the war was over. The concept of rotational warfare did not yet exist. Even with this mindset the military was able to meet the recruitment mission needed to sustain the force. A study of U.S. military recruiting conducted after the 1991 Gulf War concluded, "there is no reason to believe that the Army cannot successfully continue to maintain an all-volunteer force, as long as enlistment incentives are maintained and recruiting manpower and funding are maintained at an adequate level."[52]

The mindset of rotational warfare did not exist and yet, recruitment from 1991 to 2001 continued without any problems.

Will doing away with rotations have a negative effect on the families of deployed service members? As seen over the last ten years of combat, every family handles deployment differently. A better question might be, how do multiple one-year deployments affect families versus one single, yet lengthy deployment? Rotational deployments create a cycle of pre-deployment stress, year-long deployment stress, and reintegration stress that occurs over and over again. More stress comes as families anticipate the next deployment. Many service members already know their next deployment date within six months of returning from a deployment. Yet, there is also a great deal of stress involved in not knowing when the next deployment is. Although service members rotate home for one to two years, a RAND study on "Army Deployments OIF and OEF" describes this time at home as "the "dwell" pace that can be hectic and the hours spent at work each day, very long."[53]

Military divorce rates are also a concern. Yet, the pentagon statistic on divorce only extends back to 1992.[54] Even if statistics dated further back, it would be difficult to compare past historical numbers with those seen today. The military could not compare the divorce rate of service members during a non-rotational war such as, WWI or WWII with the divorce rate of rotational wars, OIF and OEF because of societal changes over that period. The only way to gauge the affect of rotations on divorce rates would be to compare them with the rates of a current operations conducted without rotations. The current system of rotational warfare prevents that study from happening. More studies should also be devoted to the negative effects of rotational warfare on families in order to answer the question of whether doing away with rotations altogether would have negative consequences.

The main goal of rotational warfare is to give units a chance to recover. In WWII entire units rotated to the rear to allow the leaders and troops to recover from the frontline. It was possible for units to do this because there were enough troops and units in theater to replace them. In Iraq and Afghanistan, the ability for units to rotate companies back to the rear and regroup was not possible. There simply were not enough troops and companies to replace them. The result was that every unit stayed in the fight continuously for a year with no opportunity to regroup and recover. If overwhelming force is used and maintained in the war it will give battalion and company commanders the opportunity to rotate units. With more units in theater battalion and company Area of Operations are smaller, allowing commanders to rotate companies or platoons to regroup and recover. This method will allow troops to recover while still maintaining the continuity needed to accomplish the mission quickly.

Conclusion

When Al Qaida attacked the United States on September 11, 2001, the people of the U.S. were ready to go to war. Clausewitz defines this emotional state of a country as primordial violence.[55] The longer the conflict continues the more primordial violence dies. Prolonged wars exhaust the will of the people and their treasure. Adversaries use protracted warfare as a strategy when fighting a stronger force. No other force in the world can match the U.S. military head to head and win, which is why protracted warfare is its only weakness.

Rotational warfare, a system where one-third of the force deploys, one-third trains for the war, and one-third returns home and recovers from the war is causing protracted wars. Rotational warfare limits the number of troops available for post conflict stability operations to

33% of the fighting force. It restricts planners from having adequate numbers of troops to handle post conflict security and provide basic needs to the host nation populace. Failed security leads to insurgencies and a protracted war.

Rotational warfare hinders continuity in counterinsurgency operations. Military advisors change out as units rotate and new advisors must start relationship-building all over again. Continuity also ends as new leaders rotate into the war. New leaders bring new ideas for attacking the same problem instead of continuing on the path the old unit set in place. Each new plan takes time to establish and execute. Lack of continuity protracts the war.

Rotational warfare negatively affects the mindset of military leaders and troops. Risk aversion dominates the minds of service members and leaders who know if they survive just twelve months, they will get to go home. Because units will get to return home at the end of their rotation regardless if endstate objectives are reached, the mindset of leaders is also inclined to focus more on troop morale instead of mission accomplishment. This causes leaders to mismanage manpower, assets, and money. Risk aversion and a "survive twelve month" mindset among leaders protracts the war.

The United States should re-examine its war fighting strategy and realize that by using rotational warfare it is giving the enemy the one and only weapon it has to use against it, protracted war. Sending overwhelming forces to the fight and keeping them there until the endstate is accomplished is the only way to prevent prolonged conflicts. This is how the U.S. military can remain the dominant force in the world today.

Each U.S. military branch has attempted to address the problem of rotations by adjusting the length of their rotations. LTC Parks addresses the issue in the monograph *The Unit and the Individual: A Study of Rotation of Forces in Counterinsurgency.* LTC Parks recommends different lengths of deployment based on the unit or service member's mission rather than the branch of military. LTC Parks proposes that combat units rotate after one year, but Division staff, advisors, and mentors rotate after two years.[56] Current conflicts in 2012 where the U.S. is conducting stability, security, and COIN operations could be helped by applying this strategy and also by lengthening twelve-month tours to two or three year deployments. It is possible that this method could reduce problems associated with rotations.

ENDNOTES

[1] Conrad C. Crane and W. Andrew Terell. *Reconstructing Iraq: Insights, Challenges, and Missions for Military Forces in a Post-Conflict Scenario.*

[2] Carl von Clausewitz, *On War*, ed. and trans. Michael Howard and Peter Paret, 89.

[3] FM 3-24, Counterinsurgency, ix.

[4] Norman Cigar, *Al-Qa'ida's Doctrine for Insurgency*, Potomac Books, 2009, 13.

[5] Cigar, 20.

[6] Cigar, 20.

[7] Daveed Gartenstein-Ross, *Bin Laden's Legacy: Why We're Still Losing the War on Terror,* John Wiley & Sons, Inc., July 20, 2011, 177.

[8] The Three strategies of Huang Shih-Kung agrees with Sun Tzu's Art of War, arguing that speed must be emphasized in military engagements, and that long, indecisive wars of attrition must be avoided. (The Seven Military Classics of Ancient China, 286)

[9] MCDP 1 Warfighting, 39

[10] Robert Shear and Barry Groves, Center For Army Analysis: *The Army Rotational Rules Projects*, 10.

[11] Shear and Groves, 10.

[12] Brigadier General H. R. McMaster, Director of Combined Joint International Assistance Task Force, Shafafiyat (Transparency) for International Security Assistance Force, Kabul Afghanistan, Interview with author on February 4, 2012.

[13] Lakhdar Brahimi, *Comprehensive review of the whole question of peacekeeping operations in all their aspects*, para 87, 15. "The first 6 to 12 weeks following a ceasefire or peace accord is often the period for establishing both stable peace and the credibility of the peacekeepers. Credibility and political momentum lost during this period can often be difficult to regain."

[14] Crane and Terrill, 4.

[15] Crane and Terrill, 6.

[16] FM 3-24, 1-9.

[17] FM 3-24, 1-67. "Most density recommendations fall within a range of 20 to 25 counterinsurgents for every 1000 residents in an AO. Twenty counterinsurgents per 1000 residents is often considered the minimum troop density required for effective COIN operations; however as with any fixed ratio, such calculations remain very dependent upon the situation."

[18] James Dobbins, Andrew Rathmell, Keith Crane, Seth G. Jones. And John G. McGinn, "Germany," *America's Role in Nation Building: From Germany to Iraq*, 4.

[19] The importance of incorporating the insurgents into the solution is not a mistake. In the reconstructing of Germany after WWII, the decision to work with former Nazi personnel was necessary to being able to hand over the country to the Germans as quickly as possible. The decision not to work with former Bath party members is arguably one of the biggest mistakes in OIF. Today there are signs of talks with the Taliban in an effort to incorporate the organization into the Afghanistan government and illuminate the Taliban resistance.

[20] Sir Robert Thompson, *Defeating Communist Insurgency,* Chap. 2.

[21] Hull, 34.

[22] Brigadier General H. R. McMaster, Director of Combined Joint International Assistance Task Force, Shafafiyat (Transparency) for International Security Assistance Force, Kabul Afghanistan, Interview with author on February 4, 2012.

[23] Brigadier General H. R. McMaster, Director of Combined Joint International Assistance Task Force, Shafafiyat (Transparency) for International Security Assistance Force, Kabul Afghanistan, Interview with author on February 4, 2012.

[24] Parks, 16.

[25] Major Francis J. H. Parks, *The Unit and the Individual: A Study of Rotation of Forces in Counterinsurgency*, 17.

[26] Parks, 16.

[27] Parks, 17.

[28] Parks, 19.

[29] Parks, 5.

[30] Hull, 15.

[31] Parks, 13.

[32] Parks, 13.

[33] Stephen E. Ambrose, *Band of Brothers,*237

[34] Mark Abramson, *McChrystal orders AAFES scaled back*, http://www.stripes.com/news/mcchrystal-orders-aafes-scaled-back-1.98854, Stars and Stripes, (Accessed on January 4, 2012)

[35] Joint Base Balad, http://militarybases.com/overseas/iraq/balad/ (Accessed February 16, 2012)

[36] Abramson, (Accessed on January 4, 2012).

[37] Abramson, (Accessed on January 4, 2012)

[38] Abramson, (Accessed on January 4, 2012).

[39] Crane, iv.

[40] James Fallows Interview, *Invasion of Iraq*, 1.

[41] Fallows, 2.

[42] Fallows, 2.

[43] Fallows, 2.

[44] US Department of State Website, Diplomacy in Action - http://www.state.gov/r/pa/ei/bgn/6804.htm (Accessed on February 24, 2012)

[45] Larry Shaughnessy, *Army to reduce deployment time in war zone to 9 months* http://articles.cnn.com/2011-08-05/us/army.afghan.deployment_1_army-deployments-soldiers-stress?_s=PM:US(Accessed on January 15, 2012)

[46] Michael E. O'Hanlon, and Ian Livingston, *Iraq Index: Tracking Variables of Reconstruction & Security in Post-Saddam Iraq*, November 30, 2011 (Accessed on February 24, 2012, http://www.brookings.edu/iraqindex).

[47] Doug Dubrin, *Military Strategy: Powell Doctrine*, http://www.pbs.org/newshour/extra/teachers/lessonplans/iraq/powelldoctrine_short.html (Accessed on December 18, 2011).

[48] Dubrin, (Accessed on December 18, 2011).

[49] Parks, 28.

[50] Lieutenant Colonel Darrell Duckworth, "Affects Of Multiple Deployments On Families", 5.

[51] Thomas W. Evans, *Army History: The Professional Bulletin of Army History, The All-Volunteer Army After Twenty Years: Recruiting in the Modern Era*, http://www.shsu.edu/~his_ncp/VolArm.html (Accessed on January 15, 2012), 40-46

[52] Evans, 40-46

[53] Timothy M. Bonds, Dave Baiocchi, and Laurie L. McDonald, *Army Deployments to OIF and OEF,* 22. "In fact, however, all of the time not spent in theater (i.e., "Not BOG") is counted as "dwell." That means that "dwell" includes all of the time spent traveling to theater, the time spent traveling home, and the time spent training away from home station (e.g., at the National Training Center—NTC—at Fort Irwin, CA). (Thus, rather than BOG:Dwell, the ratio might better be called BOG:Not BOG.)

A 1:1 BOG:Dwell ratio indicates that a soldier spends one time period (typically a year, and sometimes up to 15 months) in theater, and the same amount of time not in theater (including time at home station, traveling to and from theater, and training) before returning to theater. A 1:2 ratio indicates two time periods away from theater for every time period in theater, and a 1:3 ratio yields three time periods away from theater for every time period in theater. The Army has recently deployed soldiers to Iraq and Afghanistan at ratios of 1:1 or even higher. The Secretary of Defense has set 1:2 as his objective, whereas the Army prefers a sustained BOG:Dwell of 1:3."

[54] LTC Derrell Duckworth, *Effects of Multiple Deployments on Families,* 10.

[55] Clausewitz, *On War*, 16.

[56] Parks, 44.

BIBLIOGRAPHY

Ambrose, Stephen E. *Band of Brothers.* New York, NY: Simon and Schuster, 2001.

AMOS, DAVID H. PETRAEUS and JAMES F. *FM 3-24, MCWP 3-33.5, (Counterinsurgency).* Washington D.C.: Headquarters Department of the Army, 2006.

Belasco, Amy. *Troop Levels in the Afghan and Iraq Wars, FY2001-FY2012: Cost and Other Potential Issues.* Prepared forMembers and Committees of Congress, Washington D.C.: Congressional Research Service, 2009, 72.

Brahimi, Lakhdar, *Comprehensive review of the whole question of peacekeeping operations in all their aspects*, United Nations General Assembly, Fifty-fifth Session, August 21, 2000 http://www.un.org/peace/reports/peace_operations/(accessed January 3, 2012)

Ciesinski, LTC Paul, interview by Dr. Chris Ives. *Operational Leadership Experiences In the Global War on Terrorism* Combat Studies Institute, (October 13, 2006).

Clausewitz, Carl von. *On War.* Translated by Michael Howard and Peter Paret. Princeton, New Jersey: Princeton University Press, 1984.

DePu, Mark. *Vietnam War: The Individual Rotation Policy.* November 13, 2006. http://www.historynet.com/vietnam-war-the-individual-rotation-policy.htm (accessed November 22, 2011).

Dubrin, Doug. *PBS.* http://www.pbs.org/newshour/extra/teachers/lessonplans/iraq/powelldoctrine_short.html (accessed December 19, 2011).

DUCKWORTH, LIEUTENANT COLONEL DARRELL. *Affects of Multiple Deployments on Families.* Carlisle, PA: Strategic Research Project, 2009.

Evans, Thomas W. "The All-Volunteer Army After Twenty Years: Recruiting in the Modern Era." *Army History: The Professional Bulletin of Army History, No. 27* , Summer 1993: 40-46.

Fallows, James, interview by PBS. *Invasioin of Iraq* (January 28, 2004).

Fielder, David. *Defining Commander, Leadership, and Management, Success Factors Within Stability Operations.* Carlisle, PA: Strategic Studies Institute, 2011.

Foxnews.com. *Goodbye, Burger King: Top U.S. General Orders Closure of Western Comforts in Kandahar.* March 25, 2010. http://www.foxnews.com/world/2010/03/25/goodbye-burger-king-general-orders-closure-western-comforts-

kandahar/?utm_source=feedburner&utm_medium=feed&utm_campaign=Feed%3A+foxnews%2
Fworld+%28Internal+-+World+Latest+-+Text%29 (accessed January 4, 2012).

Gerras, Leonard Wong and Stephen. *The Effects of Multiple Deployments on Army Adolescents.* Monograph, Carlisle, PA: Strategic Studies Institute, January, 2010.

Groves, Robert Shearer and Barry. *The Army Rotational Rules Project.* Analysis, Washington D.C.: Center for Army Analysis, 2001.

Helton, Bradley Dean. *Revolving Door War: Former Commanders Reflect on the Twelve Month Tour Upon Their Companies in Vietnam.* Masters Thesis, Raleigh: North Carolina State University, 2004.

Hosek, James. *How is Deployment to Iraq and Afghanistan Affecting U.S. Service Members and Their Families?* Santa Monica, CA: RAND Corp, 2011.

Hull, Captain Jeanne F. *Iraq: Strategic Reconciliation, Targeting, and Key Leader Engagement.* Carlisle, PA: Strategic Studies Institute, September, 2009.

Hunt, MG James P. "The 800 Gorilla and Stability Operation." *Small Wars Journal,* 2010: 1-6.

James Dobbins, Andrew Rathmell, Keith Crane, Seth G. Jones and John G. McGinn. *"Germany," America's Role in Nation Building: From Germany to Iraq.* Santa Monica, CA: Rand, 2005.

Karsh, Mark Wilbanks and Efraim. "How the "Sons of Iraq" Stabilized Iraq." *Middle East Quarterly,* no. Fall (2010): 57-70.

Karsh, Mark Wilbanks and Efraim. "How the "Sons of Iraq" Stabilized Iraq." *Middle East Quarterly,* Fall 2010: 57-70.

Library, The American War. *Vietnam War Allied Troop Levels 1960-73.* http://www.americanwarlibrary.com/vietnam/vwatl.htm (accessed January 14, 2012).

Manwaring, Max G. *The Strategic Logic of the Contemporary Security Dilemma.* Monograph, Carlisle, PA: Strategic Studies Institute, December, 2011.

McMaster, BG H. R., interview by Major Gregory K. Gibbons. *Rotational Warfare* (February 4, 2012).

Michael S. Johnson, MAJ, USA. *The Myth of the Unsistanable Army: An analysis of Army Deployments, the All Volunteer Force, and The Army Force Generation Model.* Masters Thesis, Fort Leavenworth, Kansas: U.S. Army Command and General Staff College, 2009.

Palgutt, Colonel Kevin J. *Lessons Learned: 13 Months as the Senior Military Advisor to the Minister of Interior.* Lessons Learned, Carlisle, PA: Strategic Studies Institute, September, 2010.

Park, Francis J. H. *The Unit and the Individual: A Study of Rotation of Forces in Counerinsurgency.* Monograph, Fort Leavenworth, Kansas: School of Advanced Military Studies, 2007.

RAND. "Too Many Months of Military Deployment Can Reduce Reenlistment Rates." *RAND.* October 7, 2009. http://www.rand.org/news/press/2009/10/07.html (accessed December 22, 2011).

Record, Jeffrey. *Bounding The Global War on Terrorism.* Monograph, Carlisle, PA: Strategic Studies Institute, December, 2003.

Robbins, Eric Peltz and Marc. *Leveraging Complamentary Distribution Channels for an Effective, Efficient Global Supply Chain.* Santa Monica, CA: RAND Corporation, 2007.

Terrill, Conrade C. Crane and W. Andrew. *Reconstructing Iraq: Insights, Challenges, and Missions for Military Forces in a Post-Conflict Scenario.* U.S. Army War College, Carlisle: Strategic Studies Institute, 2003.

Timothy M. Bonds, Dave Baiocchi, and Laurie L. McDonald. *Army Deployments to OIF and OEF.* Prepared for the U.S. Army, Santa Monica, CA: RAND Corps, 2010.

West, Bing. *Statement to the House Armed Services Committee re: Afghanistan.* July 27, 2011. http://www.bingwest.com/complete_articles/congressional_testimony_july_27_2011 (accessed November 22, 2011).